Ten Days

ZAMBIA

*Chobe
Savanna Lodge*

NAMIBIA

ZIMBABWE

BOTSWANA

MOZAMBIQUE

Atlantic Ocean

SWAZILAND

Indian Ocean

LESOTHO

SOUTH AFRICA

AFRICA

Cape of Good Hope

on the Chobe

A Photographic Journal at the Crossroads of History

Published by SACOVA Publishing, Inc.
Designed and Produced by Cosgrove Associates, Inc.
Library of Congress Control Number: 2002104180
Printed in Japan by Toppan Printing Co.

This photographic journal is dedicated to:

All the members of the New York City Fire Department, past and present.

The legion of men and women who don a uniform each day in order to protect their fellow citizens.

Every American scarred by the events of September 11, 2001.

The author wishes to express his appreciation to the entire staff of the Chobe Savanna Lodge for their flawless hospitality and profound concern throughout the ten days on the Chobe from September 8th through 17th, 2001.

Ten Days on the Chobe

Photography & Text
Robert B. Haas

About the Author

Ten Days on the Chobe is the fourth photographic journal of African wildlife by noted author and photographer ROBERT HAAS. His previous books include the award-winning *A Vision of Africa* (1998), *Predators* (2001) and *African Critters* (2002). The author and his works have been featured in numerous publications and in two segments of the internationally syndicated *CNN Business Unusual*. Haas is a graduate of Yale University (1969) and Harvard Law School (1972). Since 1983, the author has been Chairman of the Board and founder of a private investment firm in Dallas, Texas, whose heritage includes a series of renowned acquisitions in the consumer products and healthcare fields. Haas is a frequent lecturer at the Yale School of Management and Harvard Law School.

The author's works have been donated worldwide to schools, wildlife conservation organizations and other charitable causes, and have been used as teaching material, a magnet for charitable contributions and an expression of appreciation for extraordinary achievements. In 2002, the United Nations Environment Programme and The WILD Foundation honored the author by presenting him with their Special Recognition Award for his literary and personal contributions on behalf of endangered species and the environment. Through his work, Haas hopes to share his passion and love for Africa's diverse wildlife with a wide audience who may appreciate the beauty and dignity of its creatures. A native of Dallas, the author has traveled extensively in Africa on photographic safaris, often joined by his wife and three daughters.

Contents

Introduction

It was not until the morning of the tenth day of our photographic safari along the Chobe River, in an area where it marks the watery boundary between Botswana and Namibia, that the idea occurred to me to create this photographic journal. The past ten days had been like no other safari we had ever taken into remote regions of Africa.

The notion of compiling a photographic journal exclusively from the photos taken, and the words penned, during a single safari of only ten days' duration had an irresistible appeal, particularly since the concept of doing so was not planned in advance of the trip. This would be my fourth photographic journal in a series dating back to 1998, each with its own distinct format and dominant theme. *A Vision of Africa* (1998), the first, reflects my earliest adventures in Africa and my earliest photographic efforts, a collage of photographs and brief quotes or passages unconnected by any well-formed constructs about African wildlife – the concept is to mirror a visitor's very first exposure to this venue in an almost random sequence of images. *Predators* (2001) focuses on the unique dynamics between predator and prey, attempting to draw a comprehensive photographic circle around the complex life cycle of African predators and thereby expand the knowledge of the reader beyond the simple notion of one animal hunting down another whenever hunger pangs dictate. *African Critters* (2002) is directed toward children, pre-readers and early readers, attempting to engage their hearts and minds in a world

where their generation will determine the fate of a host of endangered species.

Despite the varying themes of each of my photographic journals, the works are bound together by a central purpose – the desire to share the African wilderness, in vivid images and personal text, so that the reader would emerge with a greater appreciation of the beauty and dignity of all creatures that inhabit this timeless wilderness and a greater sense that our own responsibilities as a species extend to preserving this world for our children, their children and future generations.

If, then, the primary purpose of my photographic journals is to share, faithfully and intimately, the actual safari experience, why not simply invite the reader into my safari vehicle (in this case, an 18-foot dinghy) and inside my villa at night throughout the course of a span of ten consecutive days … confining the published work to the photos taken and the words recorded during that single span of time? Wouldn't that be the most genuine experience of all? The photos selected for the journal would be limited to the images captured during this period of ten consecutive days, not images that might be more artistic or more dynamic but could be drawn from other trips and other venues in Africa. The journal excerpts that form the backbone of the text would be based on the words actually penned on those ten days, working primarily by flashlight in the early morning or late evening hours, not more carefully crafted passages tapped

3

ELEPHANT
A mud-drenched pachyderm wades in at close range

PREVIOUS SPREAD
NATIVE FISHERMAN
Pausing in his mission to gather the catch that provides sustenance for his family and currency for barter in his village

out on a computer keyboard in the comfort of my study months or even years later. Wouldn't this self-limiting approach be the most faithful reflection of the experience, the one that would draw the reader most directly along as a witness to, and participant in, an actual African safari?

In light of the fact that the concept for this photographic journal did not take shape until the very end of the trip, often the passages that follow, presented in the chronological sequence in which the diary entries were written at the time, bear scant or even no relationship to the photographic and viewing experiences of that particular day. At other times, however, the passage might be more directly tied to the game "drives" in question. In an effort to draw some linkage between the journal entry itself and what was transpiring that day, certain passages are preceded by a brief "Author's Note" which provides some context for the genesis of the passage.

But even the periodic disconnect between text and photos is itself a genuine reflection of the safari experience. Countless safari-goers will attest that, in between the sensory overload of game drives, your hyperactive mind will wander across a vast

conceptual landscape without clear boundaries into crevices that partake not only of the creatures *du jour*, but also of the meaning of life, the impact of death, the bonds of family, our responsibilities to wildlife, and so forth.

This particular safari experience transpired at a single venue along the banks of the Chobe River in an area in which the River marks the boundary between the countries of Botswana and Namibia in southern Africa. The images that follow include both creatures who were "citizens" of one country and citizens of the other, and even herds of Elephants and one intrepid Lioness caught photographically in the process of swimming across the watery international border between the two. It is ironic that there is only one photographic sequence of a land-based predator in this entire journal (pictures of the water-based Crocodile and airborne birds of prey abound) — not a single Leopard peering out from behind a cloak of foliage, nor a lone Cheetah cautiously feasting on its fresh prey, nor even a Hyena or Jackal patiently awaiting its chance to scavenge a meal. Just the one Lioness furiously paddling across the Chobe in the pre-dawn hours. Perhaps there is a lesson in all this — Africa is fully capable of offering up its unparalleled beauty in a multitude of shapes, sizes and venues. The inherent dignity of its creatures and the bewildering diversity of its charms are expressed each day, with or without the added dimension of predation.

All the images published in this work were recorded during the ten-day period from September 8th through 17th (although a few rolls of film were shot on the evening of my arrival on the 7th and the morning of my departure on the 18th). But this was not just any ten days. These ten days were sandwiched around an event of cataclysmic proportions that occurred thousands of miles away – the terrorist attack on the twin towers of the World Trade Center in New York and the Pentagon in Washington in the early morning hours of Tuesday, September 11, 2001.

Once we learned, via short-wave radio, of the awful assault on American soil and American sensibilities, our plans – and our lives – changed immediately. We jettisoned our arrangements to travel into even more remote regions of Botswana and scrambled to arrange our return to the States once the ban on international travel lifted. From that moment forward, the images captured and the global events that unfurled each day were wound together tightly in a helix of conflicting emotions and deep frustrations. In view of the logistics of travel from a remote region of Botswana-Namibia to the States and our virtual isolation telephonically, the trip took on a surreal quality as we shuttled back and forth between photographic sessions and frantic efforts to locate loved ones and arrange passage home.

For generations to come, legions of literary works will issue forth on the emotional anguish and the historical impact unleashed by the terrorist assault. This journal is not intended to decipher either; it is intended only to share with the reader, photographically and textually, an extraordinary period of ten days on the Chobe.

5

WHITEFRONTED BEE-EATER
A palette in flight

HIPPOPOTAMUS
*Both sides of this behemoth
are on display – slumbering
peacefully and enraged at our
intrusion into its turf*

ELEPHANT
Blanketing the shoreline of the Chobe

GREATER KUDU
Eventually, even the most timid accept the River's invitation to slake their thirst

12

BABOON
At peace … and on alert
at water's edge

PREVIOUS SPREAD
EGRET
Embedded in a sea of fronds

13

CROCODILE AND IMPALA
*A reptilian predator approaches
two unsuspecting Impalas*

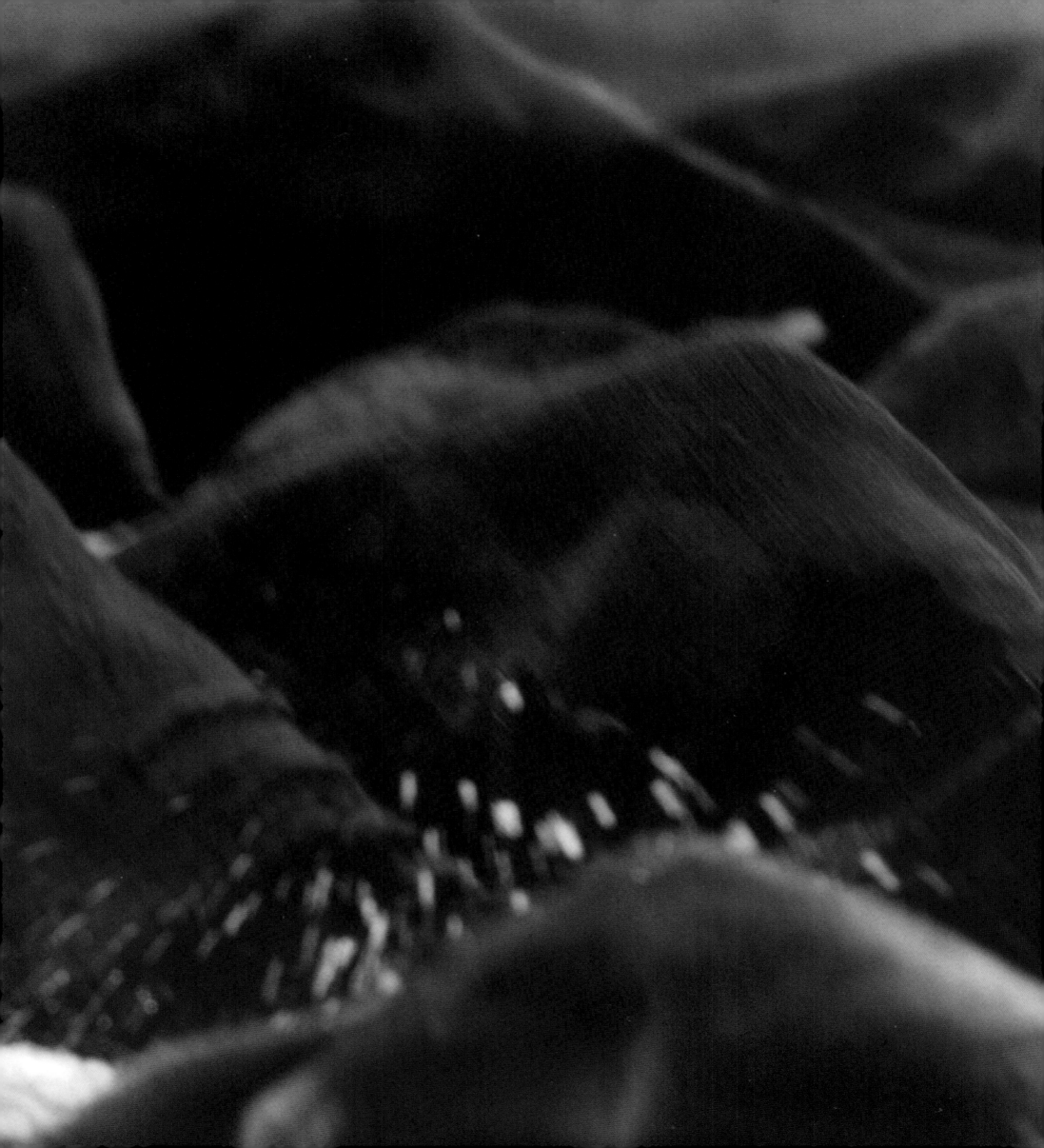

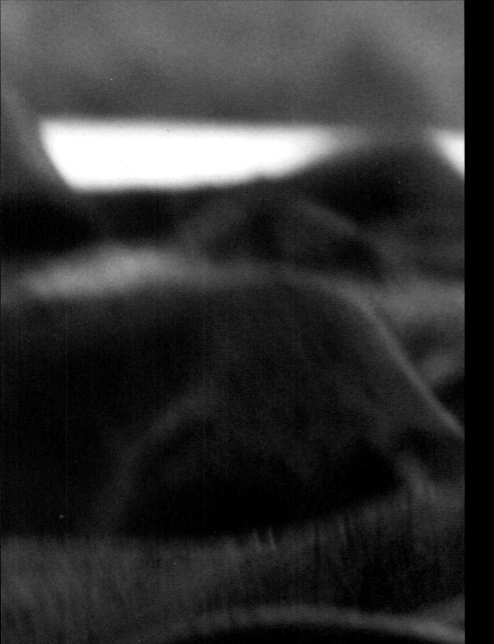

ELEPHANT AND LION
A herd of Elephants and a single Lioness cross the Chobe in faint pre-dawn light

Back to the Fron

Thursday, Septembe

It's early evening Johannesburg time on September 6th, and we've just lifted off from Hartsfield Airport in Atlanta aboard South African Air flight #210, a mammoth B-747. The steady roar of the jet engines drowns out the conversations of nearby passengers. I am alone with my thoughts as we slowly work our way across the Atlantic.

It's 0100 hours on June 6th, 1944, and we are crossing the English Channel, just a few miles west of the Normandy coast, aboard the massive but cumbersome C-47 aircraft. The heavy drone of the propellers drowns out any other sounds in the bowels of the plane. I am alone with my thoughts as we prepare to infiltrate German positions on what will forever be known as "D-Day".

I have been preparing for this day for months. It is perhaps my 12th or 13th photographic safari over the past six years. I am filled with anticipation tempered with just a trace of anxiety at the prospect of being in the water exposed to perhaps hundreds of wading Elephants and who knows how many Crocs and Hippos, the latter invisible beneath the surface of the Chobe River.

I have been preparing for this day for months. It is my first mission; for many of my brethren, it will be their first and last. I am filled with dread, tempered with just a trace of anticipation, at the prospect of being on the beach or floating beneath my parachute ever so slowly to earth, exposed to German soldiers, invisible inside their machine-gun nests.

Perhaps I am just a middle-aged man engaged in games better played by boys.

Perhaps I am just a boy engaged in a battle better fought by men.

I am younger in spirit than my years with dark black hair and facial features unusual for someone in his 50s.

I am older in spirit than my years with features too harsh for someone in his 20s.

My arms still ache from lugging aboard all my gear weighing over 50 lbs. – three camera bodies with power boosters attached, four lenses of different shapes and sizes, filters, over 200 cartridges of film, 56 extra batteries, flash attachment, power converter, remote shutter switches, film-safe lead pouches, four extra battery magazines, 1.4x and 2.0x magnifying converters, brushes, a canister of Dust-Off, manuals, lens extender, stabilizing metal platforms, monopod, waterproof plastic sacks, cleaning kits, ...

My shoulders still ache from lugging aboard all of my gear weighing over 50 lbs. – main parachute and harness, back-up chute, machine gun, grenades, ammo, plastic explosives, bayonet, K-rations, emergency rations, cartons of cigarettes, canteen, insulated vest, flashlight, maps, gas mask, helmet, knives, extra clothes, life jacket, utensils, shovel, first aid kit, ...

The popular misconception of a photographer armed with just a camera and a vest filled with rolls of film is just that … a misconception.

The popular misconception of a soldier armed with just a rifle and belts of ammo is just that … a misconception.

There's an old saying that the best shot is the one you're not prepared to take.

There's an old saying that the worst shot is the one you're not prepared to take.

Frozen in my seat on the way over, I wonder whether all my experience from the past will fade when I am face-to-face with my subject. Will my shutter finger hesitate just a bit when it is time to perform its appointed task?

Frozen in my seat on my way across the Channel, I wonder whether all my training will desert me when I am face-to-face with my enemy. Will my trigger finger flinch just a bit when it is time to perform its appointed task?

Only time will tell how well I'll perform under pressure. While there is clearly some element of risk in what I do, it is rarely a matter of life and death.

Only time will tell how well I'll perform under pressure. While there is clearly some element of adventure in what I do, it is first and foremost a matter of life and death.

ELEPHANT
A rare moment of solitude
for a member of the herd

PREVIOUS SPREAD
CROCODILE
Even an artistic shade of blue
fails to mask the sheer menace
in this hunter's stare

SQUACCO HERON
A sharp-eyed fisherman with
the quarry securely in its beak

MONITOR LIZARD
With an extended family that includes
the fearsome Kimono Dragon

ELEPHANT
A feisty young bull at play proudly trumpets his conquest over a more passive herd-mate

OPPOSITE
HIPPOPOTAMUS
Direct eye contact is easily
induced by entry into its
safe zone

SEQUENCE ABOVE
EGRET ON HIPPOPOTAMUS
This family of Egrets has
booked safe passage on a fleet
of floating barges

FOLLOWING SPREAD
IMPALA WITH ELEPHANT
Peaceful coexistence
between two grazing herds

Feeling Civilized

Saturday, September 8, 2001

Author's Note   At the end of the first full day of photography with my mentor and fellow photographer Richard du Toit, I reflect on the changes that have overtaken me.

After over 30 hours of travel (by commercial and charter flight, jeep and boat), four immigration and customs checkpoints, and passage from the U.S. to South Africa to Botswana and finally to the Namibian side of the Chobe River, I reached the first of my three scheduled safari destinations. Late Friday afternoon, with only two or three hours' sleep in the past 36 hours, Richard and I dumped our duffels at the main lodge in order to catch the last few vestiges of sunset. In a virtual daze by 10:00pm, I unpacked and literally collapsed in the sack half-clothed for my first night's rest.

Throughout the morning and late afternoon on Saturday, we pressed hard on the Chobe, hampered by a thick fog that would no doubt impress its murky shroud on our images. Later in the trip, with a passel of solid rolls in our vest pockets, we would be inclined to cut this day short and focus only on exceptional shots where the subject would dominate over the compromising conditions. But on our first day, we did not have the luxury of knowing whether the shroud would be our constant companion. Fatigued to the point of having no appetite, I bowed out of dinner and retired to my villa early.

With three or four hours to myself, I switched gears, propping my legs up on the bed and savoring a more leisurely pace. Freshly showered and sipping a Windhoek Lager for dinner, I realize that I have changed one world for another. Jetliners have been traded in for the sight of a river boat carved from a single log, the frantic pace of the business day has become a slow drift down the Chobe toward a Fish Eagle on a neutered branch, the multi-headed dragon of daily priorities has lost all but one head … at last, I am feeling quite civilized, once again.

39

BUFFALO
Always the same greeting
from this ungracious host

OPPOSITE
PIED KINGFISHER
One thin reed provides an
observation deck for this
agile fisherman

PREVIOUS SPREAD
ELEPHANT
Nursing mother well protected
by a garrison of sentries

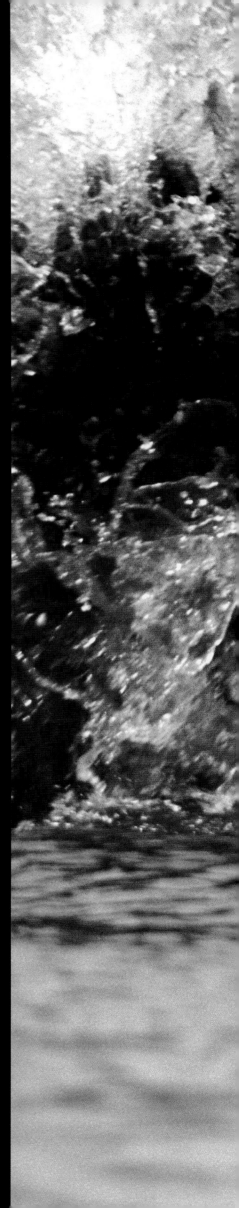

HIPPOPOTAMUS
SEQUENCE AT LEFT
Mother at play with her
amused offspring

RIGHT
Two wide-eyed adults
in a furious territorial
joust … the fun is over

CROCODILE
Calm waters appear to
double the headcount of a
solitary predator

44

45

GIANT KINGFISHER
SEQUENCE ABOVE
A vigorous headshake sheds
water and lifts plumage

SEQUENCE BELOW
This toothy prey will eventually
be swallowed whole

The Eye Still Sees
What It Wants

Sunday, September 9, 200

SEQUENCE ABOVE AND RIGHT
YELLOWBILLED STORK
*A graceful predator silently
approaches … dives … and
flips its tiny captive between
brightly colored mandibles*

PREVIOUS SPREAD
HIPPOPOTAMUS AND DARTER
*African Darters stand guard
over a well-camouflaged Hippo*

Early morning on my second day on the border between Botswana and Namibia, and I am sipping java while being serenaded by the territorial calls of two distant Lions. After a "normal" night's rest of almost six hours, I feel as if I am just beginning to get my physical and photographic bearings, once again. In contrast with virtually all other professional photographers, I practice my trade only three times per year in Africa on safaris that last anywhere from 10 to 15 days. In between, I may shoot a dozen rolls or so back in the States, usually just to break in a new piece of gear or to test the old pieces right before a trip. During the prolonged hiatus between trips, my gear rests idly on the shelf and my photographic skills atrophy from lack of use.

Yesterday was my first full day in the field since the end of May, a gap of over three months. And unlike the professional athlete who greases his return to action with the ointment of spring training and the warm-up of exhibition games, my first day out "counts" every bit as much for me as a playoff game does for him. On my first morning, I may see (as I did yesterday) two Hippos breach the water simultaneously and "kiss" mouth-to-mouth in midair. I never saw that before, and I have no idea when (or even whether) I'll see it again. I believe I got the shot (the answer lies somewhere inside a spent film cartridge), but there was no trial run to hone my somewhat rusty skills for that moment.

Within another day or so, I should feel back in fighting trim. But those first few days back are a conscious struggle to marshal my resources, with game drives punctuated with episodes of fumbling to remove a 1.4x converter, vainly attempting to mount the flash attachment inside out, forgetting to activate my quick control dial when I switch to manual mode, and so on. If it weren't so serious, it would be quite comical. At least, I'm gradually learning not to be quite as harsh on myself as I used to be. If I lose my composure, it will just take longer to find the groove. And after years of this same hit-and-miss pattern of returning to action, I've come to realize that the results of those early game drives have not turned out to be quite as disastrous as I once feared. Even on my best and most fluid days, batteries run low, film needs to be changed, cameras wobble and the sun disappears ... all at the wrong time. It's just part of the trade.

But there is one piece of gear in my arsenal that needs no dress rehearsal ... it is ready for action from the very start. It is my eyes – the photographer's compass, the drill sergeant who barks out orders to the raw recruits in crude terms that need no translation. Indeed, that is their only role: to define the mission, spot the target and compose the image for capture. My eyes decide whether it's better to shoot the herd of Elephants from the side or front, to call for the short lens or the long, to anticipate the action before it ever happens. And their judgment must be made in a split second. These are not mountains we're shooting ... our subjects charge and dive and take wing.

It takes my eyes little time to hit their stride upon my return to Africa. Well before my fingers are adroit at finding the right exposure or locking in on a subject in motion, my eyes will visualize what they want. Subject, background and composition are processed in my mind's eye almost from the start. In the first day or so, my eyes issue orders that the rest of my skill set cannot quite execute. Like the aging boxer whose mind writes checks that his body can no longer cash, my eyes find the target before I am quite ready to capture it.

The explanation for my ever-ready set of searchlights is rather straightforward. I use my eyes every day for reconnaissance missions ... their regular duty includes not just routine tasks but also the more specialized assignments involved in other aspects of my photographic life: culling through thousands of pictures after each safari, selecting candidates for specific roles in my next published work, reviewing design spreads and matchprints with a surgeon's precision.

Eventually, my other skills close the gap and, when all the elements are in sync, I feel on top of my game. Until then, it is a bit of a frustrating minuet in which the dancers are somewhat out of step.

51

BABOON

The almost human antics
of a troop of Baboons

BABOON
Confrontation between two
evenly matched bantamweights

56

AFRICAN SKIMMER
The peculiar disconnected bill
of this insistent chick will
evolve into the trademark fishnet
of its attendant mother

ELEPHANT
An industrial-strength dust bath leaves its distinctive mark

FOLLOWING SPREAD
HIPPOPOTAMUS
Reflective sunlight from a hazy sky offers a brilliant backdrop to this massive yawn

It Was a Good Death

Monday, September 10, 2001

VULTURE
*Silhouetted scavengers
maintain a patient vigil*

Author's Note   September 10, 2001 ... the day before the terrorist assault on New York and Washington. For reasons that will never be entirely clear in my own mind, I awoke just before 4:00am with an irresistible urge to write at length about the subject of death. It is not unusual for me to feel compelled to write in the middle of the night. The timing is good – a few hours' sleep have refreshed the body and awakened the imagination. And the venue is ideal – the pitch-black African night and the exotic calls of nocturnal hunters are downright inspirational. But, with the benefit of hindsight, this particular writing episode is eerily ironic. Inspired by an account of how young men faced the prospect of death in World War II, the passage below delves intimately into this subject to an extent that is at once both painful and comforting. It follows a winding course along a personal journey that stretches from the bedside prayers of my childhood to medical crises of more recent times. I embarked on this journey just one day before an entire nation and indeed the whole world would have reason to take a similar journey.

Today

I will finish reading *Band of Brothers*, Stephen Ambrose's account of the exploits of the men of Easy Company, 101st Airborne Division, tracing their daring exploits from the invasion of Europe on D-Day, June 6, 1944, to the occupation of Hitler's Eagle's Nest almost one year later on the eve of Germany's surrender. It is nearly impossible to immerse yourself in this absorbing description of how young men, boys really, faced and often succumbed to death on the beaches of Normandy or on Hell's Highway or in Bastogne without wondering at times, "How would I have handled such circumstances?". Crouched down in a foxhole, shivering in a wet poncho with mortar fire overhead, would I have been a dedicated soldier, a cowardly deserter or just another casualty amongst the grisly carnage?

The answer is that I'll never know for sure. The best that can be said is that perhaps there are a few faint hints in my own life tracks. All we can do is to examine how we may have viewed the prospect of death, not from the safe distance of hypothetical self-examination, but rather in the context of "close calls" that have invaded our comfort zone of seeming immortality.

Over the years, I have spent a great deal of time thinking about death, my own death. Even as a young boy, I would lie awake in bed for hours, aware that one day I would lie in total darkness and total silence without the prospect of being rescued by the morning. Each night, our last words spoken aloud would be this bizarre bedside prayer that was so common in those days:

> *Now I lay me down to sleep,*
> *I pray the Lord my soul to keep.*
> *If I should die before I wake,*
> *I pray the Lord my soul to take.*

How could this little ditty have become so popular for our generation? It's a wonder that I slept at all in my childhood.

In later years, I managed to survive a series of brushes with death. In my late 30s, there were two epileptic seizures while driving on the freeway – once missing a concrete bridge abutment by a few feet and the other time emerging with only a bloody nose when I collapsed face first into oncoming rush hour traffic. I have no recollection of the second incident, but recall hearing the details from the paramedics in the ambulance.

A few months later, after a CT scan, a rather aloof and pompous brain surgeon delivered his clinical opinion (in an operating prep room within earshot of other patients) that I had a brain tumor

ELEPHANT
Synchronized slurping

almost the size of a golf ball, which appeared to be malignant. For the remainder of his dissertation on the origin and development of brain lesions, I just stared glassy-eyed at the hideous pattern and colors of his sport coat. The surgeon concluded with the news that "we" would operate the next morning and attempt to remove the offensive mass while leaving my mental and speech faculties "reasonably intact". At last, I heard the words: *"Any questions?"* Since "we" were planning to operate, I turned to my new surgical colleague and announced that we would not be operating tomorrow. Dumbfounded, the

brain surgeon asked, *"And why is that, Mr. Haas?"* Very calmly, I replied, *"Because no one who wears a sport coat like that is going to drill holes in my head."*

After hours of firing probing questions at a team of neurological specialists (which did not include the surgeon of dubious sartorial taste), I still was not satisfied that my symptoms indicated, with sufficient clarity, the presence of a malignant brain tumor. But the options were quite limited: either perform the surgery immediately and biopsy the removed lesion (risking permanent impairment to my mental faculties) or delay the surgery for a period of months in order to perform further tests and observe the progress of the mass over time (risking the further development of a potentially malignant tumor). By a split vote (I cast the deciding ballot … I guess the only ballot), the newly constituted "we" decided to postpone the surgery.

Six months later, the lesion was slightly but noticeably smaller in size (malignant tumors do not shrink without the intervention of aggressive treatment) and the official verdict was in: *arterial-vascular malformation,* a twisted mass of blood vessels in the brain which formed the lesion from traces of blood that had seeped out and calcified over the years. Not exactly a pleasant condition, but not a death sentence either. Over time, the mass would cause some abnormal neurological episodes, but it would eventually break up as the calcified deposits detached from the central mass.

The six-month period between the original "malignant" diagnosis and the eventual verdict of clemency was simultaneously the most awful period of my life and one that would "sweeten" the flavor of the balance of my remaining years. No matter how optimistic you remain during this period, there is no responsible choice other than "arranging your affairs", both personally and financially, for the worst possible outcome. Feeling at times like both the lead actor and an observer in a scriptless play, I watched others as others watched me. There was always a very distinct sense in their eyes that they were observing a soon-to-be ghost. No one said, but everyone thought, that my calm demeanor was either a full-blown case of denial or a stiff upper lip in between sessions of emotional breakdown. In truth, it was neither – I simply never believed that the lesion would turn out to be malignant. Naturally, I had my doubts but never to the point where I lost the conviction that this would pass. Eventually, I had one convert to the cause. Candice [my wife] finally declared: *"I know you … you will heal yourself, you will make it go away."*

In contrast to someone who has no prospect of reprieve from a death sentence, my stoicism could not be attributed to either emotionless resignation or incredible bravery. I was confident that ultimately I would be spared, but I was also acutely aware at times that I could very well be mistaken. For six months, I had the luxury of focusing on death as a life stage without knowing whether this exercise fell under the heading of "crisis management" or "long-term planning". In retrospect, this episode in purgatory was a two-sided mirror that exposed both the best and the worst sides of life at the same time. The prospect of death would never again be banished to the dark recesses of a closet, only to be opened much later in life; and the beauty of things living would never again be taken for granted.

In the end, I emerged with my own distinctly personal philosophy about the privilege of life and the role of death inherent in that privilege. That philosophy is not a full-fledged recipe but only a list of ingredients (some convictions and others just questions). It is a recipe that works for me but may be tasteless for others. Its sound bites are neither original nor healing:

> *No one gets out of life alive.*

> *At a funeral, we mourn less for the deceased than for ourselves and for the others left behind.*

> *A life devoted to evading death is a battle destined to be lost.*

> *There may be a certain grace and dignity in our heroes dying young … they are forever preserved in youth and beauty and excused from the indignities of old age.*

In the final analysis, I place great stock on the circumstances surrounding death. The killing of the members of Easy Company during WWII is swathed in valor and heroism; the death of a drunk driver on a binge partakes of neither. Our Native American ancestors fervently believed that death on the battlefield or in pursuit of adventure is to be revered, not mourned. I am often reminded of one of the closing lines from the film *Legends of the Fall* when the Native American mentor of Brad Pitt's character describes his death at a ripe age at the hands of his old nemesis, a grizzly bear, in the words, "It was a good death."

CARMINE BEE-EATER
This dashing hunter offers up a captured bee as a courting gesture and, once accepted, consummates the act

CROCODILE AND FALLEN LOG
Life imitates bark

71

BUFFALO AND BUFFALO CARCASS
*Contemplative bull seemingly
mulls over its inevitable fate*

Pushing the Limit

BUFFALO
Beady eyes and beaded nostrils
strike a combative pose

PREVIOUS SPREAD
ELEPHANT
Peach-fuzzed toddler beside its
mother's protective bulk

Author's Note   The passage below was recorded in my safari journal at 5:30am local time on September 11th, roughly nine hours before the terrorist attack on the World Trade Center and the Pentagon half a world away.

In film jargon, "pushing the film" refers to the technique of setting your camera for a "faster" film than you've loaded in the camera. Faster film requires less time exposed to sunlight to record the image. While slower film takes more time, it is also capable of recording more "information" and therefore better color saturation and tonality. The idea behind "pushing the film" is to allow you to shoot high-speed action with slower film.

Sometimes in the field, we push our own limits as well. Yesterday was just such an occasion. In two separate sequences, we "pushed" the action beyond what common sense might dictate. In the first instance, we came across two massive Hippos wading peacefully in a rather shallow inlet attached to the Chobe River through a narrow channel. Even though we could easily have reached the pair with our long telephoto lenses from the relative safety of the Chobe, our view would have been partially blocked by the riverbank that separated river from inlet. So we slowly maneuvered our 18-foot motorboat through the narrow channel and directly into the inlet. The view was now totally unobstructed, and we burned film to our heart's content. Occasionally, we shifted position and changed lenses in order to modify our perspective. Although we moved with the utmost caution, the reality is that we were sharing this bathtub with two very hostile and gargantuan rubber duckies.

Only after we had sated our appetites and withdrew from the inlet did it dawn on us that, if either or both of the behemoths had mounted a charge, we would have been trapped. There was no way our boat could have reversed its way through the channel in time to escape an irate charging Hippo. We would no doubt have been upended and landed in the drink, at the mercy of our pursuer.

An hour or so later, we stationed ourselves along the banks of the Chobe about 50-75 feet west of a lineup of roughly ten Elephants wading knee-deep in the water and enjoying an afternoon drink. We were well positioned photographically with the afternoon sun on our backs. In this case, we were not in harm's way at all … that is, until the Elephants gradually shifted positions further and further to the west, just a few feet at a time. The pace of our motor drives quickened noticeably as the pachyderms' images engulfed our entire viewfinders. We shot, up close and personal, at a range where even individual eyelashes and toenails were easily distinguishable in the frame. Once again, we were mesmerized by the images beyond the point where we would have had adequate time to escape a hostile charge. Our craft was literally beached in the sand less than ten metres from the herd, our engine cut in order to avoid the vibrations affecting our focus at such close range. We had allowed ourselves for the second time in two hours to drift well inside the zone of a "clear and present danger."

On each safari, we somehow manage, either unwittingly or witlessly, to push the edge of the envelope, if not the edge of the post office. We are not proud of such moments; in fact, in retrospect, we are a bit mystified by our own lapses in judgment. When we do so, I would like to believe that it is neither the product of conscious bravado nor photographer's extremism. We simply lose ourselves in the moment, unable to turn away from shots that are becoming more dramatic by the moment. Until either we have had our "fix" or one of us snaps back to reality, we are guilty of extracting our own bodies from the scene at hand. For just a fleeting moment, we convince ourselves that we are some kind of invisible observers, when in fact we are quite visible trespassers on their turf.

Just as "pushing the film" is a technique of marginal value, "pushing the film-maker" is a technique of suspect judgment. Upon reflection, it hardly seems worth the risk … but then those images come back from the developer ….

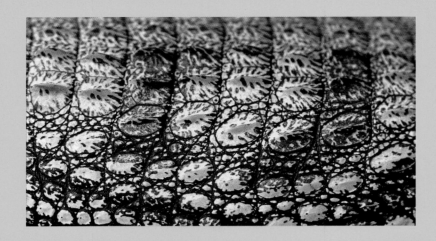

CROCODILE
*Bits and pieces and the business
end of this toothy stalker*

80

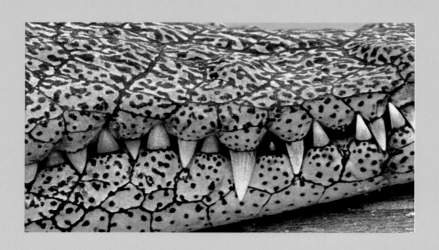

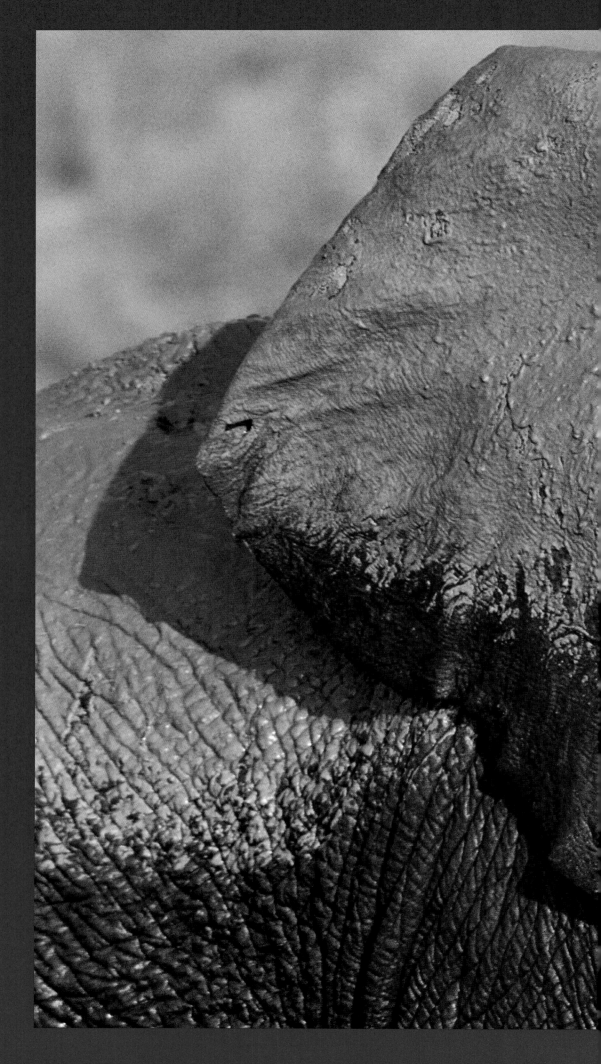

82

ELEPHANT
Laser eyes emerge from
behind a muddy shroud

HIPPOPOTAMUS
It's only a matter of time before
open jaws and piercing glares
erupt into battle

FOLLOWING SPREAD
ELEPHANT
*A thirsty herd puts
on a trunk show*

LEFT AND BELOW
ELEPHANT
*Eyelashes and toenails
captured at close range*

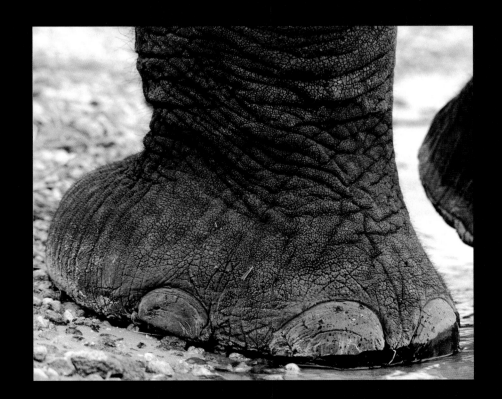

The World Has Changed Forever

Wednesday, September 12, 2001

Author's Note   With the six-hour time difference between our location along the Chobe River and the Eastern shores of the States, the terrorist assault took place just before 3:00pm local time on Tuesday, September 11th. At that hour, fellow photographer Richard du Toit and I had just begun our afternoon session on the River, returning at our customary time shortly after sunset. We trudged back to our separate villas for a brief shower before dinner, reconnecting to the rest of the world through our short-wave radios. After absorbing the shockwave that awaited us, my pen fell silent and my journal remained closed until the following afternoon.

It's less than 24 hours after the terrorist attack on the World Trade Center and the Pentagon … and the world has changed forever. Last night at just after 7:00pm, Richard and I walked along the stone path that connects the crude pier where we beach our craft to the individual thatched-roof villas. Weighted down by heaps of photographic gear and the canisters of film that contain our hoped-for catch-of-the-day, we exchange the carefree banter of those who are unaware that a seismic shift has taken place.

Minutes later, Richard burst into my villa clutching his short-wave radio tightly in both hands. Until that moment, I always thought the phrase "he looked like he had seen a ghost" was just a timeworn cliché. Not any more. Richard gently set the short-wave on the end of my bed, as if dropping the receiver might sever our only remaining link to the outside world. We both listened in absolute silence as the BBC announcer delivered the news of the terrorist attack in a voice that sounded like an excerpt from a 1940s newsreel. The individual words simply did not fully register in my mind, but the overall message did. I do remember my mouth being wide open and my shoulders slumping visibly as if I had just absorbed a vicious blow to the stomach.

Once I digested the shockwave of the news, it dawned on me that [my wife] Candice, [and daughters] Samantha and Vanessa might all be in the Manhattan area. I simply could not remember in those first frantic moments whether Vanessa was back at Yale from the weekend horse show and whether Candice would have already left for California to join [our daughter] Courtney for the Rosh Hashonah holiday. I was not functioning on all cylinders – I was too isolated geographically and telephonically to click into gear. Then we remembered that Andre, the lodge manager, possessed the only cell phone in the area. Richard and I located one of the staff, who pointed out the way to Andre's home, located about 800 metres from the lodge.

I recall a host of vivid sensations during that 800-metre walk through the darkness: it was long, terribly long … Richard was silent, but I was mumbling … we stumbled often and several times almost fell into huge holes that had been dug to plant trees … the faint twinkling light from Andre's home never seemed to get any closer.   Only in retrospect do I realize that this general area was populated by a large herd of Buffalos and that a pride of five Lions hunted at night in the vicinity; one night, the Lions had killed a total of five Buffalos in virtually a nonstop feat of mayhem.

Eventually, we reached Andre's home and he surrendered his cell phone without a word. In the background, there were images on his TV of an airplane crashing into a skyscraper. After a few frustrating minutes of busy circuits and static-filled reception, I reached my assistant Christine. I figured that I might only be able to make a single call under the circumstances and that if I got through to Christine, she would be able to report on the whereabouts of the entire family. Finally, I heard her voice and I blurted out, "Tell me about my family!" In very calm and measured tones, Christine assured me that she had already spoken to Candice and everything was fine. All four – Candice, Samme, Courtney and Vanessa – were accounted for and unharmed. Vanessa was already back at Yale, and Courtney was safe in California. Candice and Samme were together at the St. Regis Hotel in New York, by this time surrounded by security personnel.

At this point, I broke down and sobbed. I tried to find my voice, but it was lost somewhere inside my shuddering chest. I heard a voice shouting through the receiver: "Bobby … Bobby … are you still there?" I mumbled something to Richard who stood a respectful few feet away. I remember Richard giving a "thumbs up" sign once I conveyed the news from Christine. I forced her to report, over and over again, on the whereabouts and well-being of the family. Once we gave up trying to connect via Christine to Candice in New York, I dropped the receiver to my side. Richard and I embraced; he literally held me up as I slumped forward.

Over the next several hours, I was able to reach Candice, Samme and Vanessa via a connection through Christine. Only Vanessa cried uncontrollably but her lack of control resurrected mine. Candice remained eerily calm, despite the fact that she and Samme were just a few miles from Ground Zero. Eventually satisfied that the entire family was unharmed, I returned to my villa and reassembled my senses bit by bit.

It is ironic that the very seclusion I seek when I go to Africa has turned against me … the isolation from the "normal" world has become an involuntary prison. Now I am trapped half a globe away … all international flights into and out of the States have been cancelled 'til further notice. Its borders have been sealed. We have already decided to ditch our plans to travel to Tsaro and Savuti, destinations in even more remote regions of Botswana, completely out of reach of any cell phones or fax machines. For now, we will stay at Savanna Lodge, where Andre's cell phone affords one tenuous connection to the Western world. We will be able to follow the news on our short-waves and connect telephonically from time-to-time when reception allows and the lines are open.

In the relative calm of our bunker along the Chobe, immune from the barrage of nonstop images of devastation, I begin to draw some perspective around the ragged edges of this event. This will be my children's JFK assassination, an event so sudden and awful that it will obliterate a large zone of innocence and optimism in their psyches … and in mine. The relevance of all other events has been flat-lined. The collective clamor, and need, for swift and harsh retribution will prove irresistible. The realization will seep in that the threat posed by international terrorism is a full-blown survival threat. Individual hijacked aircraft are mere slingshots compared to the biological and tactical nuclear weapons that may find their way into the hands of terrorists. This drama will play out one day at a time for years to come, but in contrast to other crises (Oklahoma City, Lockerbee, the East African embassy bombings), the ripples from this one will not fade with time. We may debate forever who is responsible, what should be done in response, etc., etc., etc. But one thing is for sure: *The world has changed forever.*

ELEPHANT
*Dueling bulls barely
warrant a glance from
nonchalant herd-mates*

98

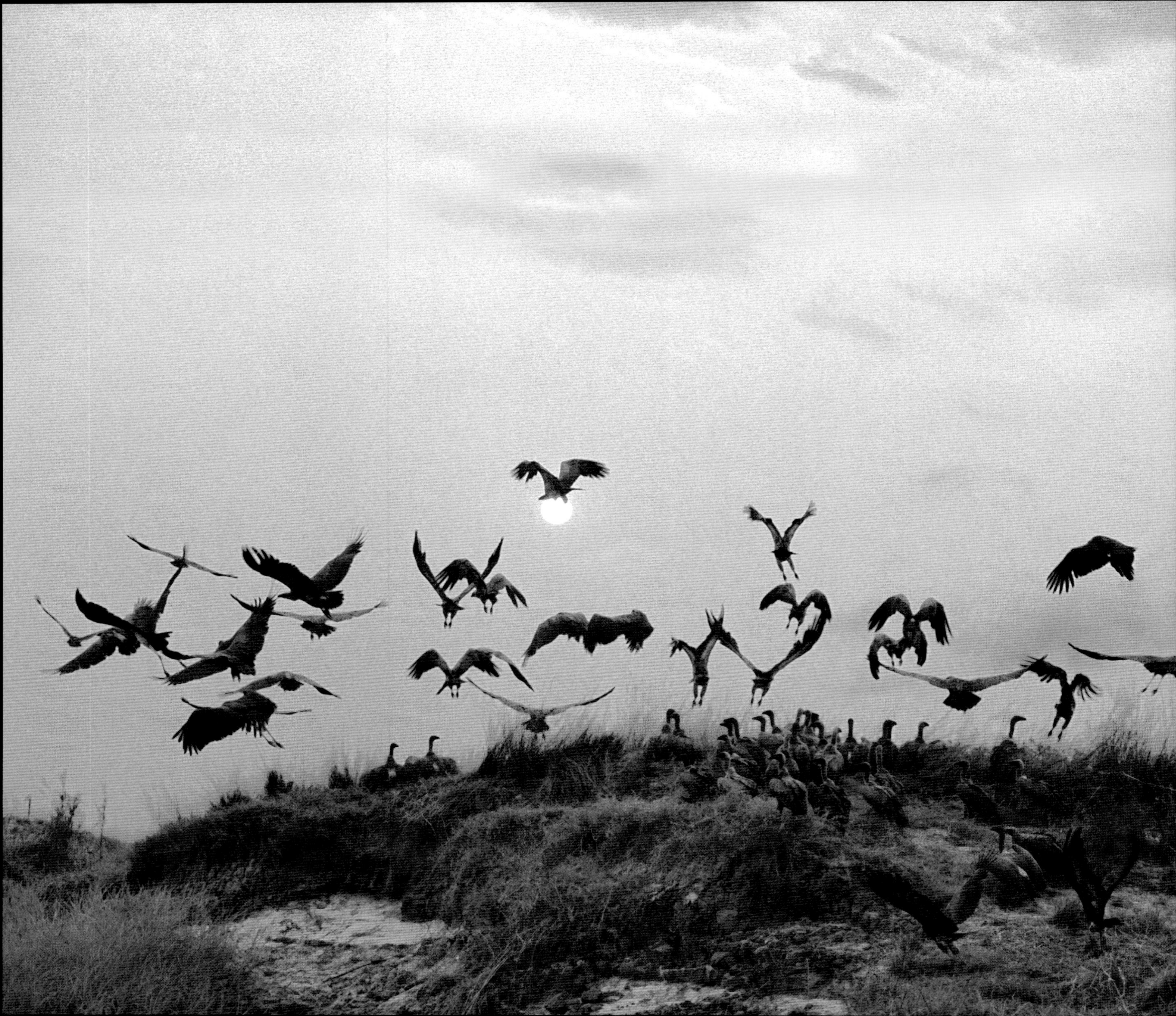

IMPALA
Bachelor herd in flight

ABOVE AND RIGHT
ELEPHANT
*Eventually, the herd clears away
and leaves a more private bank*

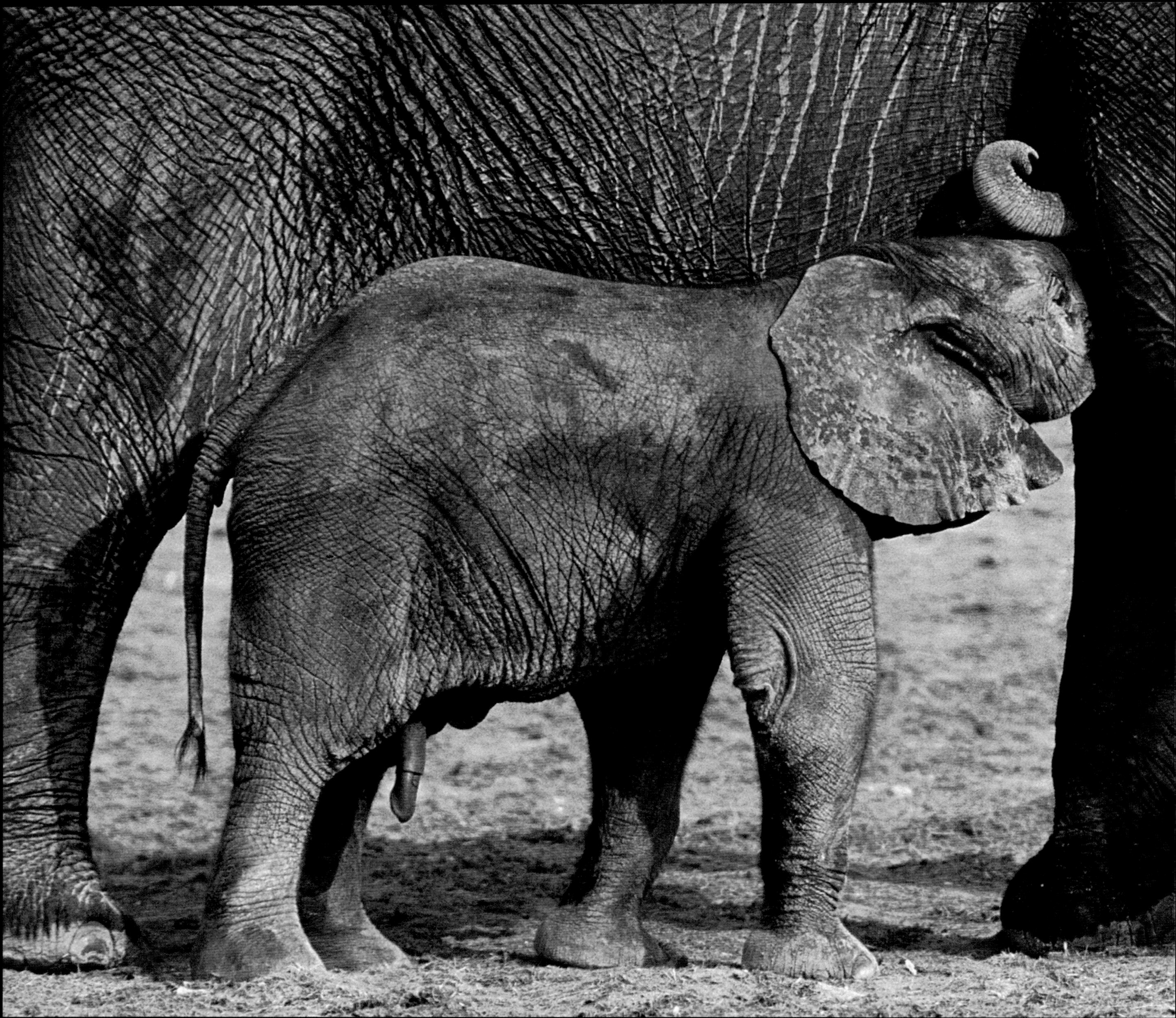

A Day of Conflict

Friday, September 14, 2

NATIVE FISHERMAN
*Gathering his nets in the early
morning light ... a trade handed
down for generations*

Author's Note   Three days after the terrorist attack, we are stranded in Namibia, and Candice is still stranded in New York. With the ban on international travel still in effect, the prospect of an early return to the States is not yet under consideration. Each day has become a bizarre twist of emotions – the Chobe still offers refuge from the events that have rocked the world, but the refuge is short-lived and laced with a heavy dose of frustration. At the end of the day, I reflect on the whiplash of emotions during the past 12 hours.

At 5:45am, Richard and I are sipping our second cup of coffee, with muted expectations that the Chobe will deliver, once again. In the faint pre-dawn glow of Africa, the awful tragedy of the Tuesday terrorist attack loosens its grip just a notch. There is a sense of unreality to the disaster – we are not subjected to the bombardment of never-ending images of impact and then collapse or the nonstop news coverage as the country gropes to find its bearings. I wonder whether the solitary fisherman gathering in his nets on the Chobe River is even aware of what has transpired.

Andre [the lodge manager] rushes into the main villa, offers up his cell phone and breathlessly tells me that I must call Christine [my assistant] immediately, that she called Andre's mobile number three times in the middle of the night and left messages on his recorder.

Just moments before, Richard and I chatted about the fact that Candice should be leaving New York this afternoon for Dallas where she would regain her footing emotionally, reunited with the clan of family canines and safely distant from the terrorist war zone.

The news from Christine is not good. A handful of suspects have been taken into custody for attempting to board a commercial aircraft by impersonating airline personnel. Spooked by the incident, Candice has decided to cancel her return flight. I tell Christine to arrange a private flight for Candice as soon as humanly possible.

Unable to control events in the States any further, Richard and I head for the dock and our belated departure down the Chobe in the direction of the soon-to-rise sun. The carefree swagger of boys at summer camp is noticeably absent, but we carry on for lack of anything else to do. Within 15 minutes, our spirits are aroused as we are treated to the rare sighting (and filming) of a large Lioness swimming from one side of the Chobe to the other, paddling furiously to evade any underwater attack by a silent and invisible Croc – the terrestrial King of Beasts has literally crossed the border into the kingdom of another where it is no more than an edible subject. After blasting two complete rolls apiece during a sequence which lasts only two or three minutes, Richard and I are aware that we have just witnessed a terribly special sighting, accented by a spirited Lioness who repeatedly snarled and blew plumes of spray on her way across from the Namibian side to the shores of Botswana.

Moments later, we spot a second Lioness on the banks of the Chobe, and we prepare ourselves for an encore performance ... seven hours later, we are still waiting. As clouds roll in and the light begins to fade, we abandon our position.

On the way back to Savanna Lodge, we come across a herd of roughly 100 Elephants, spread along the banks of the Chobe and scattered in the hillside above. The scene is absolutely surreal. In order to capture this tableau from an ideal vantage point, we beach our craft on a tiny island across from the Elephants and haul our gear to the crest of a small hill. The scene is simply breathtaking.

In the process of changing film, we notice that the current has swept our boat away from the beach ... it is slowly drifting down

113

the Chobe, leaving us stranded on the tiny island. Our predicament is a tad dicey: It is late afternoon, there are about 100 Elephants across the Chobe fully capable of wading across to the island, we are at the very spot where one of five Lionesses launched her crossing a few hours earlier (and we are not sure of the whereabouts of the other four), and the surrounding waters are infested with Crocs and Hippos.

In a tribute to the dazzling allure of the Elephant sighting, I press my eye back on the viewfinder and expend the last few frames on my roll of film, blissfully unfazed by our loss of transportation. I then notice that our intrepid guide Richwell has dived into the Chobe in pursuit of our craft. His heroic recovery is uninterrupted by any hostiles, and we are back in business.

Deprived of further sunlight and with our energies depleted, we return to camp, knowing that inside our spent cartridges of film, we may well carry the fruits of photographic conquest. In more "normal" times (perhaps a thing of the past), we might consider the day a roaring success. But normalcy is not to be found at Savanna Lodge or anywhere else for that matter. It is a strange thing, but when we are on the water surrounded only by the works of nature, our spirits lift immeasurably; when we return to land among the manmade structures, our mood darkens and the exhilaration melts away. Today is no exception. Within an hour of our return to camp, we are brought rudely back to earth: All power in the camp is on the blink, the cell phone has lost its ability even to receive any calls, only ice-cold water flows from the showerhead, and I am reduced to writing this entry with the aid of a weak flashlight. It's been a bittersweet day, a day of contrasts. The flavor of what would normally be considered scenes of unparalleled beauty has been soured. Hopefully, the images that we have captured on film will resurrect that beauty without any bitter aftertaste. Perhaps tomorrow will be a better … or worse … day.

LIONESS

A rare glimpse of the supreme hunter – immersed in the Crocodile's domain and vulnerable to attack from an unseen predator

CROCODILE
Whether open or closed,
this vise exposes its lethal grip

ELEPHANT
During the dry season when water is less plentiful elsewhere, the Chobe attracts a ritualistic daily visit

ELEPHANT
*A teenage tantrum draws scant
attention from his elders*

ELEPHANT
*Refreshing mud baths cool the hide
and leave an artistic residue*

ELEPHANT

Amidst a forest of trunks and legs,
toddlers wrestle and roughhouse
on the banks of the Chobe

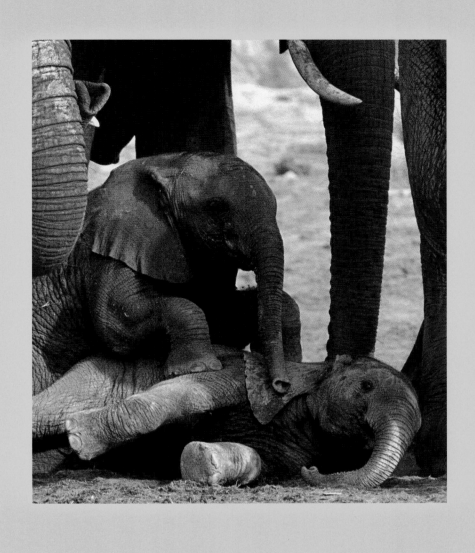

125

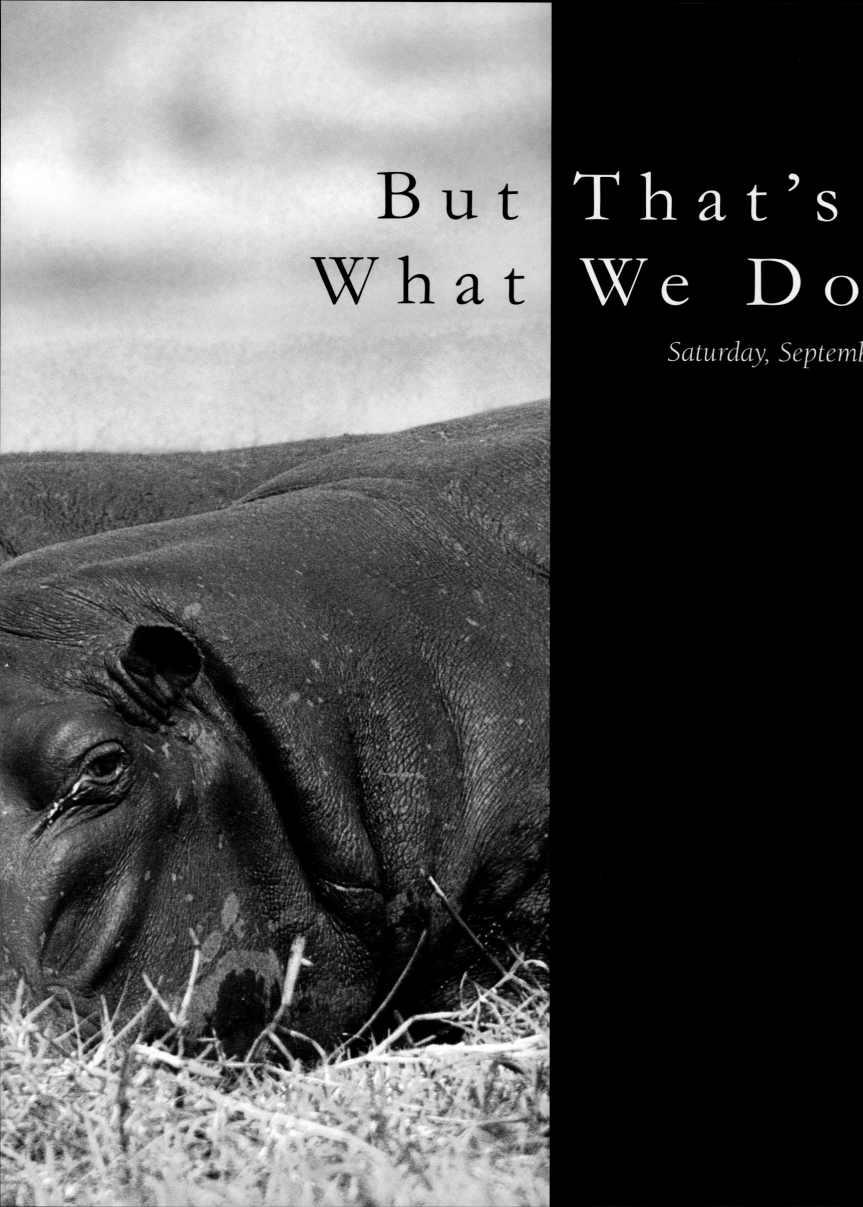

But That's
What We Do

Saturday, September 15, 2

HIPPOPOTAMUS
*A cavernous jaw from which
escape is not often negotiated*

PREVIOUS SPREAD
HIPPOPOTAMUS
*Communal napping, but their
guard is never down*

The end of another long day, and the mood has changed markedly over the past 72 hours or so since we learned of the terrorist attack. The normal carefree exuberance of our photo-orgies has succumbed to the Chinese water torture of news from the States, nonstop efforts to extract Candice from New York, and finally frantic arrangements to cobble together an early return to Dallas via Botswana and South Africa. Through no one's fault, the ambience of the trip has deteriorated into a series of photo sessions punctuated by a staccato pattern of crises. The only time we are able to escape the foul breath of a world in crisis is when we are literally on the boat, surrounded by our gear and in search of our next subject. Even then, however, we are distracted from the task at hand … unfortunately, we are operating in a venue where momentary lapses can be fatal.

Late this afternoon, after a series of rather humorous shots of a pod of Hippos at rest and at play, we scanned the gun-metal gray waters and shoreline for another subject. High winds and chilly air have evidently combined to quell the action. After drifting for 10-15 minutes, we spot another "scrum" of Hippos, several in the water and the rest standing on the banks of the Chobe. There is nothing very remarkable about this group at all, and we have already harvested more than our fair share of Hippo shots. But we stop anyway, more out of habit than in hot pursuit of a keen shot. We then proceed to make three successive passes at the group that is still on *terra firma* at the River's edge. Each pass is closer to the shoreline, but the agitated Hippos never crash into the water as hoped for. We pay no attention at all to the group that is already in the water, alternately surfacing and submerged from view.

We abandon the site after the third pass and are easing our way out to deeper waters when one of the members of the group whom we have ignored breaches the surface and explodes within ten metres of our boat. Richwell jams in the throttle, and we accelerate but the Hippo (already at full tilt) breaches again, this time within two metres of the boat. This Hippo is in hot pursuit, and we are its prey. Facing the stern of the boat with camera poised, I bomb off four or five shots as the irate Hippo breaches a third time. Then I notice the expression on Richard's face … it is one of sheer terror. Only then do I realize how close we have come to a true disaster. In our preoccupation with the shore-based Hippos, we managed to neglect the whereabouts of their underwater brethren who were apparently incensed by our three successive passes.

We motor away to relative safety, but we are both shaken up. We came close this time … very close. As I tried to photograph the Hippo's final breach, I noticed that there was a palpable sense of malevolence in its face. This was not a false charge, but a full-fledged attack that fell just short. I exhale slowly and remark to Richard, "God, that was close!" In response, Richard weakly comments, "Yeah, we could have been killed … but that's what we do." There was neither bravado nor resignation in Richard's remark, simply an acknowledgement that there is risk in what we do. Particularly in the case of Hippos, that risk is almost impossible to assess or predict. The risk is submerged below the surface, and inscrutable eyes hardly provide any clues as to what will happen next.

We are both silent for quite a while. I think about Richard's comment: "… *but that's what we do.*" Somehow, neither one of us is terribly satisfied with that explanation. It's a bit too glib … and a bit too true.

HIPPOPOTAMUS
The more gentle side of a giant ...
gazing at an Egret, kissing in midair
and dozing in calm waters

HIPPOPOTAMUS
Eyes constantly on alert

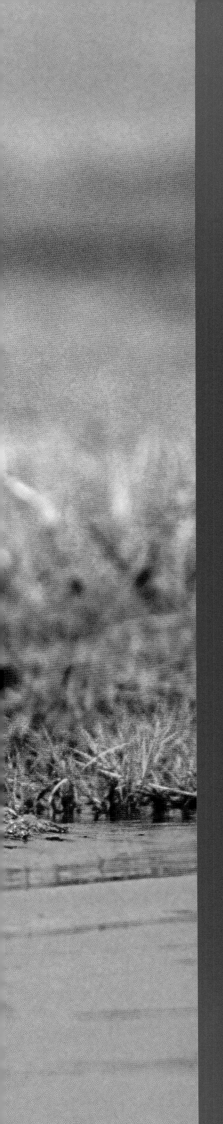

HIPPOPOTAMUS
A Hippo's gaping lunge is a
mesmerizing sight ... enjoyable
only from a distance

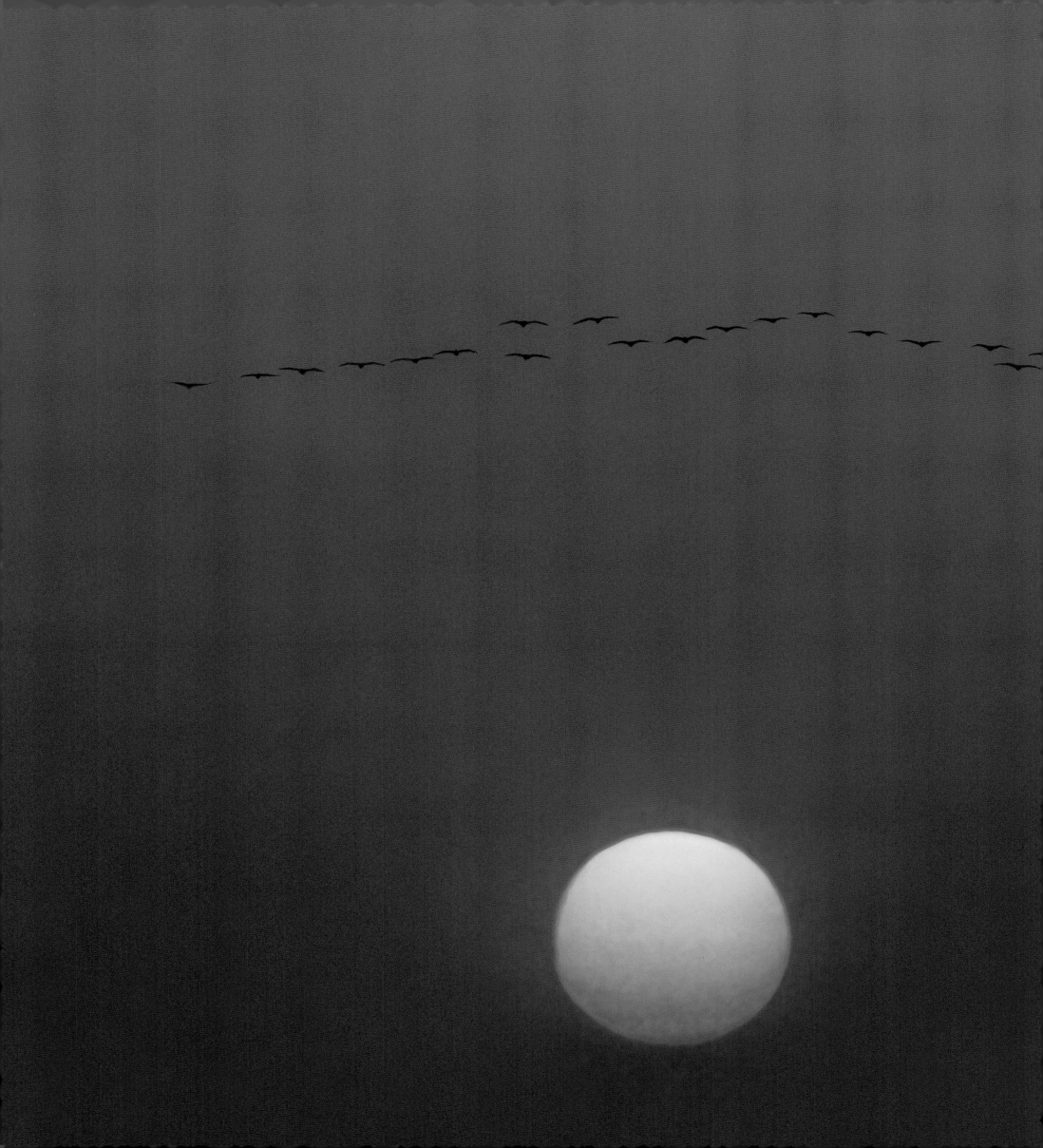

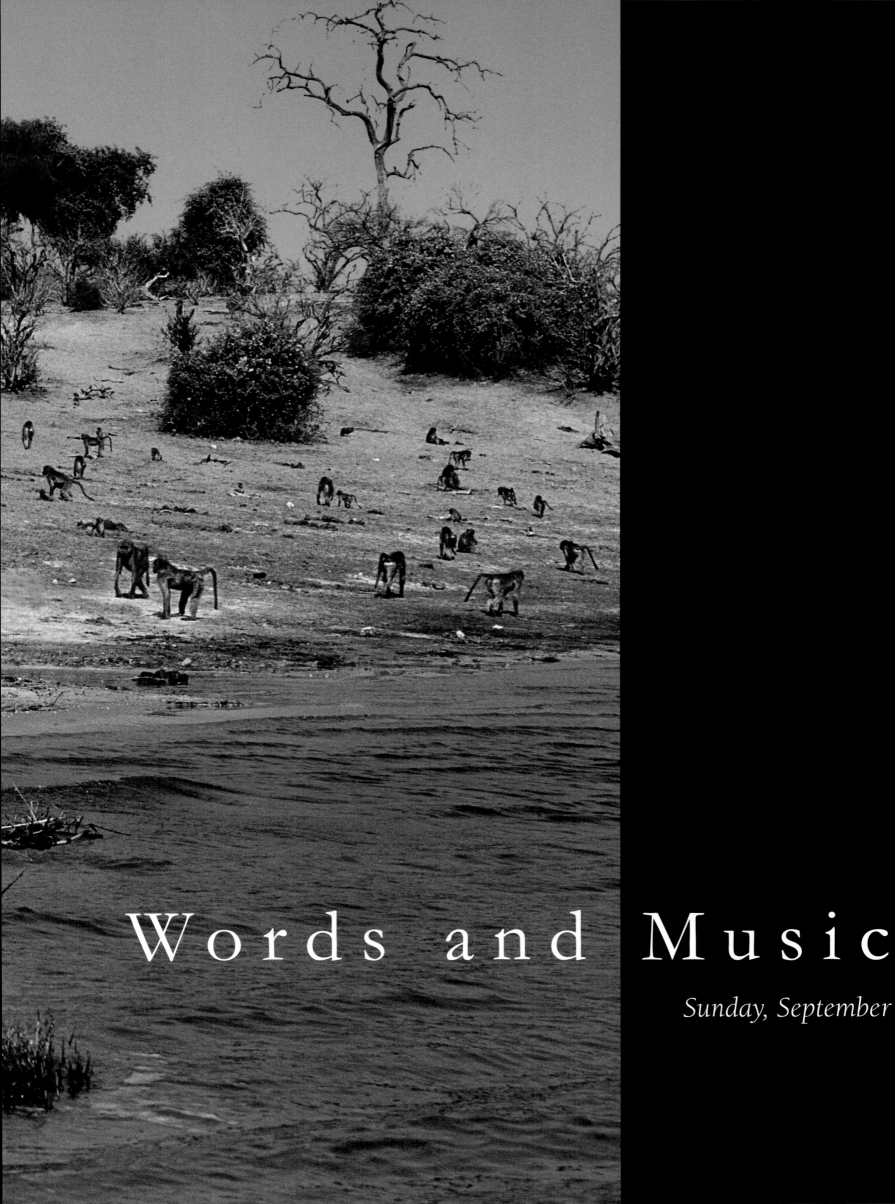

Words and Music

Sunday, September 16, 200

PREVIOUS SPREAD
IMPALA, BABOON AND CROCODILE
Kilwezi Bank offers refuge
to an unlikely assortment
of characters

ELEPHANT
Sunlight streams through
a cascading waterfall

Author's Note   On the heels of the harrowing Hippo confrontation Saturday afternoon, my feelings are more ones of guilt than of adventure. In the aftermath of the loss of thousands of lives that never bargained to be casualties in this terrorist war, I have lost my appetite for placing my body at risk simply in pursuit of a photo. I have lost my edge, and it is time to return home.

Whenever

I'm on safari, I read 25 to 50 pages each afternoon or evening just to clear my head and give my photo-saturated brain a rest. The past few days, I have been wading through a 300-page book which styles itself as an account of "true stories" from an African safari guide. What I hoped would be a shared experience from a kindred soul has deteriorated into a Buck Rogers (or, for the younger generation, a Luke Skywalker) version of the safari experience. Page after page is chock-full of one "near death" escape after another – rampaging rogue Elephants, bloodthirsty Lions, charging Rhinos and wounded but lethal Buffalos adorn each and every passage. Even if every single incident is fundamentally accurate or even wholly unembellished, the overall portrayal is distorted and a disservice to the genuine African safari experience.

All raconteurs of safari life (myself included) are unable to resist the temptation to include just a few incidents of heart-thumping danger. Indeed, a very real component of the allure and magnetism of this lifestyle is the fact that man is a trespasser here amongst behemoths and beasts – a foreign and modern element introduced into an ancient world in which foreigners are met with suspicion and outright hostility. For that reason, your behavior must be dictated not by the testosterone levels of a macho guide but by relatively simple rules of common sense. The most basic one: *Except in the most unusual circumstances, just stay in the jeep.* If this 300-page tome I am slogging through were purged of "close encounters" while on foot, it would rapidly shrink to the page count of a comic book.

Why do safari guide-authors almost always feel compelled to dwell on the "near death" version of this lifestyle? In part, it is to cater to the author's (or the publisher's) notion of "what sells"; in some measure, it is to allow the author to beat his chest gorilla-style in order to dazzle his audience. Some dose of the "dangerous anecdote" spice does add a tart and tangy flavor to the safari literature recipe. But when one hair-raising escapade after another is stapled together, the account degenerates into a distorted mish-mash which is no more genuine than is *Animal House* as a depiction of college life.

For that reason, I have found that my love of Africa is best shared with others primarily through photographs. The lens allows this author of photographic journals to impart drama, beauty and confrontation in its purest form without inserting myself into the *dramatis personae.* By definition, if I'm snapping the shutter, I can't be in the picture. Africa is an experience best shared visually … the safari experience requires mostly eyes and ears. The richness of this world-like-no-other can be fully absorbed with only the most minimal dialogue.

In my published work, I attempt to use words primarily to enhance the tonality of the photos and to lend composition to the image. At times, I, too, have succumbed to the occupational hazard of inserting a "pinch of danger" into the recipe, but it is not the main course. Each of my photographic journals is a blend of the textual and the visual (*"words and music"*), but the visual must always dominate in this symphony. We are depicting, first and foremost, a visual world.

So, too, in the world of music; if auditory brilliance dominates, we may listen to Bach or Beethoven or Rachmaninov; if words dwarf the melody, we are stuck with "rap".

145

OPPOSITE
WHITEFACED DUCK
A vigilant flock reflects
on the surroundings

ABOVE (CLOCKWISE FROM UPPER LEFT)
A bevy of aerial artists at rest
Yellowbilled Stork ... Squacco Heron ...
African Darter ... Giant Kingfisher

148

ELEPHANT
A forest of periscopes
detects an intruder's scent

FOLLOWING SPREAD
ELEPHANT
Playful pachyderms
crash into the Chobe

LEFT AND SEQUENCE BELOW
PIED KINGFISHER
Hovering in search of prey ...
diving at its target ...
emerging empty-beaked

WHITEFRONTED BEE-EATER
Arranged in a showcase
of dazzling hues

Postscript

Author's Note   A few weeks after returning to the States, I reflect on the visual and emotional landscape of my safari and contemplate the task ahead of creating a photographic journal that will capture the essence of ten extraordinary days.

By Tuesday, September 18, 2001, we had secured a charter flight from Kasane, Botswana, to Johannesburg, South Africa, and South African Air had resumed its flights to the States. Not until the eve of my departure did the thought occur to me that the experience of the last ten days should be recorded as its own photographic journal. So much had been crammed into this brief period of time: *Emotionally,* it had run the gamut from the agony of missing family members against the backdrop of terrorist rubble to the vibrancy of life on the Chobe; *photographically,* it had spanned a herd of over 100 behemoths drinking along the Kilwezi shoreline to a single Pied Kingfisher with its fishy prey secure in its beak; and *logistically,* it had leaped across centuries as we drifted by day among native fishermen in dugout canoes and scrambled at night to reconstruct travel plans via a single cell phone.

Over the past two weeks, I have transcribed the entries in my journal onto a computer disk in order to prepare the text for eventual publication. In the process, except for only minor editing, I have preserved the exact words written at the time in order to remain faithful to the overall purpose of the project itself. It is odd but this process of transcription has taken almost exactly ten days to complete. On a note of exquisite irony, during this "second" ten days, my mood has undergone a series of fluctuations that almost precisely mirrors the emotions experienced during the original ten days from September 8th through September 17th – starting out with great anticipation only to be deflated in midstream and ending in melancholy self-reflection. By the end, the creative juices had stopped flowing, blunted to a standstill by a battering of emotions.

At times, I have had misgivings about publishing this journal. It must not ever be interpreted as an attempt to place the terrorist assault in perspective – that must be left to historians and to our own individual consciences. It must also never become a backhanded attempt to capitalize on tragedy – the fact that all proceeds from my published works have always found their way into wildlife conservation causes should absolve me of this sin. In the final analysis, this journal is quintessentially personal. It is an attempt to record and recapture, through my lens and my pen, exactly what transpired during an episode that will forever be a watershed period in my life. If it serves no other purpose, just one copy of this journal resting on the shelf in my photo room will have preserved the essence for me of those ten days on the Chobe.

161

OPPOSITE
Photograph of author
by Richard du Toit